MW00901896

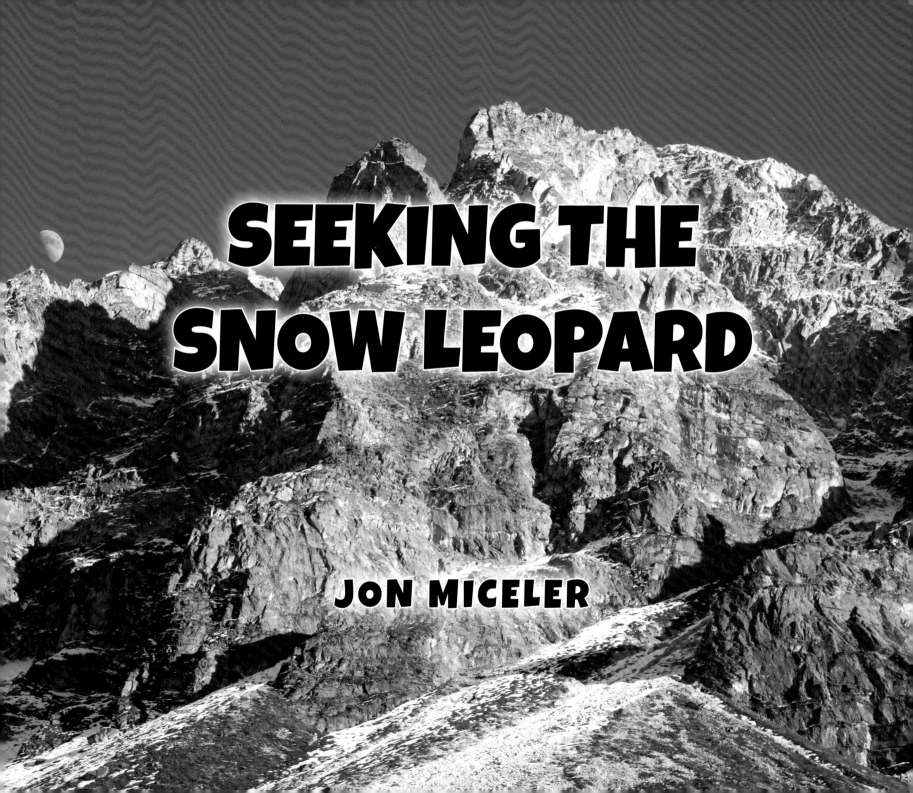

SEEKING THE SNOW LEOPARD

JON MICELER

Copyright © 2016 Jon Miceler

All rights reserved. No part of this book may be used or reproduced, stored in a retrieval system, or transmitted by any means — electronic, mechanical, photocopying, recording or in any manner whatsoever without written permission from the publisher except in the case of brief quotations embodied in critical articles and reviews.

For further information, contact:
Tumblehome Learning, Inc.
201 Newbury St, Suite 201
Boston, MA 02116
http://www.tumblehomelearning.com

ISBN 978-1-943431-16-8
Library of Congress Control Number: 2016950595

Miceler, Jon
Seeking the Snow Leopard / Jon Miceler—1st ed

Photo Credits:
Dirk Collins/WWF - Copyright & dedication pages and pages 1, 2, 10, 12, 14, 15, 19, 22, 23, 44
John Farrington/WWF - Back cover image
Jon Miceler/WWF - Pages 11, 13, 18
WWF, Nepal - All other pages
Douglas Brown (Anchorage, Alaska), September 2015, public domain Flickr - Front cover image
Chen-Hui Chang 張辰卉 - Illustrations on pages 6, 10

Design: Yu-Yi Ling 凌羽儀

Printed in Taiwan

10 9 8 7 6 5 4 3 2 1

for Yvonne Shanti
in expectation of her own future adventures

Tumblehome Learning and Jon Miceler are proud to donate a share of proceeds from this book to the World Wildlife Fund, Nepal.

Copyright 2016, All rights reserved.

TUMBLEHOME | l e a r n i n g, Inc.

WWF   World Wildlife Fund

We shall not cease from exploration, and the end of all our exploring will be to arrive where we started and know the place for the first time.

- T. S. Eliot

November 25, 2013. Eastern Nepal, the foot of Mt. Kangchenjunga.

I snap awake in the frozen darkness of my tent to the urgent blare of my radio transmitter. A trap has sprung! I worm out of my sleeping bag and pull on layers of long underwear and down jackets. I fix my headlamp to my head, unzip the tent and roll out into a swarm of my fellow biologists' lamps moving like fireflies around our dark camp, readying for the sprint up the mountain.

Running in winter at 15,000 feet in the dark morning hours of a Himalayan valley is fun for the first five steps or so. Then your body remembers you are three miles above sea level, and it gets hard to breathe. It's like running through thick mud with a plastic bag over your head and bowling balls strapped to your feet. But now we ignore such pain and run on with heavy packs, following the radio signal that indicates which cliff-side trap has sprung. A blizzard of thoughts swirls in my head as I scramble over boulders and kick steps into patches of steep frozen snow, higher and higher. What have we caught? Will the animal be injured? Could it possibly, finally, be—our snow leopard?

October 30, 2013. Bhadrapur airport, southern Nepal.

As I step from the cramped twin prop plane onto the tiny runway in southern Nepal, I am met with a furnace-like blast of hot, tropical air. We quickly load barrels with enough food for two months, warm clothes and a small mountain of technical radio-collaring gear into our vehicles. Then we begin driving two days north towards the mountains where the road ends and the trek to our snow leopard basecamp begins. Our goal is a rocky meadow at the base of the glacier fields of the world's third highest peak, Mt. Kangchenjunga. Our expedition to capture a snow leopard in the high Himalayan mountains, attach a satellite transmitter collar around its neck and let it go is the first of its kind in the Himalaya. We are excited but nervous.

3

We chose 28,169-foot Mt. Kangchenjunga for this snow leopard expedition because the mountain sits directly on the border of three countries—China to the north, India to the east and Nepal to the west. The mountain's great glaciers provide water to all three nations. Its cliffs and crags shelter the snow leopard and its prey. By tracking a snow leopard's movement with the satellite collar, we hope to show that our snow leopard uses all sides of the mountain as it searches for food, shelter and mates. This discovery, we hope, will convince all three countries to join together to protect the snow leopard and its habitat.

Mt. Kangchenjunga from Darjeeling, West Bengal, India by Marianne North (1830-1890)
Courtesy of Kew Royal Botanical Gardens

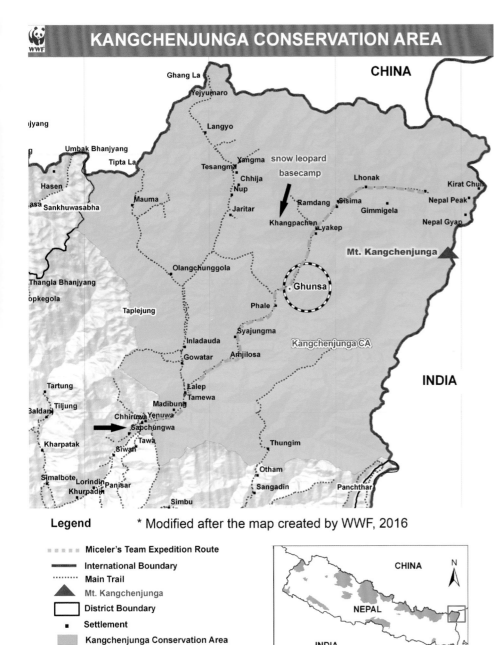

KANGCHENJUNGA CONSERVATION AREA

Legend   * Modified after the map created by WWF, 2016

- Miceler's Team Expedition Route
- International Boundary
- Main Trail
- ▲ Mt. Kangchenjunga
- ☐ District Boundary
- ■ Settlement
- Kangchenjunga Conservation Area

Mt. Kangchenjunga sits in the middle of the great Himalayan range, which starts in Pakistan and stretches east through India, Nepal and Bhutan, ending finally in the northern tip of Myanmar. All of these countries border the Tibetan areas of China to the north. The mountain range is about 1,700 miles long, about the distance from New York City to Denver or New Delhi to Mandalay or Beijing to Kunming. The highest mountain in the world, Mt. Everest, sits just to the west of Kangchenjunga.

The Himalayan mountains are young and still growing. Today if you hike in the Himalaya you can find fossils of underwater sea creatures from an ocean called the Tethys Sea, which existed before the Himalaya were created. The Himalaya began rising about fifty million years ago, when the landmass that today is India started to crash into the Asian landmass. The uplift of the Himalaya is continuing today.

The Himalayan range can be thought of as a set of giant stitches that have sewn all of these countries, shown in the map above, together. The mountains have served not as a barrier between cultures but rather as a passageway between them, connecting people, water and animals. The glacial ice of the Himalaya and the nearby Tibetan plateau contain water used by over a billion people. The snow leopard is the mystical guardian of these glaciers.

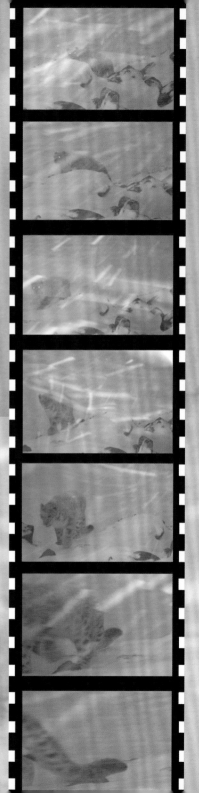

Scientists believe there are about 6,000 snow leopards living in high ranges of Asia. These mountain monarchs have evolved so they can exist right at the boundary between rocky alpine meadows and glaciers. Unlike sleek leopards of the tropics, snow leopards are heavily muscled cats made not for long sprints but for leaping down from rocky perches onto their food of choice—the blue sheep. Their bushy tails, often longer than their bodies, are perfect balancing tools that enable them to move gracefully along steep cliff walls.

Snow leopards are so rare, the local people of these high ranges have nicknamed them "Ghosts of the Mountains." Mountains protect snow leopards from hunters. But today, because the planet is warming, the leopards' mountain home is changing. The high glaciers they live near are melting, and no one knows if the snow leopard will be able to adjust to the increasingly warm climate across the mountains of Asia.

scrape

scent spray

track

pugmark

scat

In order to protect the snow leopard, we have to understand what it does every day. But no human being can follow a snow leopard through the mountains. Scientists climbing to the snow leopard's high mountain habitat must prepare well. We have to bring lots of food and warm clothes and live in tents for months on end. Even after doing all this, we are unlikely to spot a snow leopard, because their black-and-white fur coats blend in so perfectly with their surroundings. Traditionally scientists have had to rely on spotting footprints, collecting scat and observing the scrape marks left in places leopards use as a toilet. Snow leopards leave these marks to let other leopards know they have been there.

Scientists also use camera traps to study snow leopards. A camera trap is a small camera that sits in a transparent, waterproof box and automatically takes a photograph of everything that moves in front of it. Immediately after arriving in the Kangchenjunga area, we set up twenty camera traps in places we think snow leopards like. They give us photos that would be impossible to take any other way.

WCP 7 Adult Female   WCP 8 Sub Adult   WCP 9 Sub Adult

To identify the snow leopards we see on camera traps, we examine the color patterns we see on their fur coats. Like your fingerprint, every snow leopard has a completely unique spot pattern.

The easiest way to study snow leopards is to put a special satellite collar on the cat. These collars have little computers in them that transmit signals every few hours to a satellite circling planet Earth which then sends the signal down to our computers to show the leopard's exact location. These signal movements are called GPS waypoints. This allows us to peek into the private life of a snow leopard, to learn where it goes and understand how to design parks that best protect it. The really great thing about these collars is that they are programmed to pop off automatically after a set amount of time, usually about 18-22 months.

November 13, 2013.

Finally our journey by road ends. One by one our team of biologists and porters depart on the hiking trail and are swallowed up by the jungles of Nepal's lowlands. It will take us a week to hike to our snow leopard base camp at the foot of Mt. Kangchenjunga. The walking is hard, hot and sometimes dangerous as we cross rivers on bamboo tunnel bridges or sometimes on foot where bridges are too old to cross. The trail steepens each day as we go up and up.

November 6, 2013. Gyabla, Nepal.

After five days of walking we cross above treeline. The landscape changes. Mornings and nights are cold. We see snow on the lower peaks of mountains that reach 20,000 feet. The culture changes too. This is the world of mountain people, mostly Buddhist nomads, people who herd yaks and goats for a living. Their brightly colored prayer flags mark the high passes. They believe that when the wind blows through them, the prayers printed on the flags spread blessings to all people of the world. They believe this entire region is a sacred place and that water, trees, animals and mountains all have very real spirits within them. The people treat all elements of nature with respect.

We begin to encounter snow. There is less oxygen now as we walk above 13,000 feet, and our porters struggle under their loads. Soon we will be saying goodbye to these men who have carried our supplies for nearly a week into the mountains. They are anxious to get back home where the weather is warmer.

We finally reach an alpine meadow, located over 15,000 feet above sea level. Here we will make our camp for the next month. A stream runs by, providing water. A local nomad camp will sell us fresh yogurt, cheese and meat. In the afternoon, as the sunlight warms the upper snows of Kangchenjunga, we listen to the distant rumble of avalanches tumbling down.

The World Wildlife Fund has a long history of working with local communities of people that have lived in the shadow of Kangchenjunga for generations. These men and women are the real protectors of this Himalayan environment. They understand that protecting the environment is the same as protecting themselves.

Himali is the local leader of the snow leopard conservation committee. When he was a young boy, Himali worked with his family as a yak herder. He did not like the snow leopard because it sometimes killed their yak for food. After working with WWF, Himali learned that the snow leopard is an important part of nature in the mountains. If protected, snow leopards can attract tourists, who bring money to his village. Himali learned ways of living together with the snow leopard and became its greatest protector. He learned how to set up camera traps and how to trap, radio collar and release animals. He knows snow leopards so well he can even tell if a snow leopard has used nearby rocks as its toilet just by the smell.

When we arrive, we begin to set up leg traps that can catch a snow leopard without injuring it. Himali leads us to a yak path high above our camp. Photos from camera traps set up by Himali before we arrived confirm that snow leopards use this path. Snow leopards often use the same paths used by people and yaks because the walking is easier.

We set up the first foot trap. Dr. Rinjan Shrestha, a Nepalese snow leopard biologist, digs a shallow hole in the middle of the path. He places the trap trigger pad gently on the bottom of the hole. He attaches the pad to a spring connected to a metal cable. One end of the cable forms a loop, which he places on top of the trigger pad. The snow leopard first steps through the cable loop onto the trigger pad, which then releases the metal spring that instantly tightens around the snow leopard's foot.

Rinjan anchors the cable firmly to iron rods buried in the ground to hold it in place. We all place large rocks over these rods to insure the captured snow leopard does not pull the whole trap out of the ground. Lastly, we place small twigs, moss and dirt over the cable loop to disguise the trap. Everything is now ready.

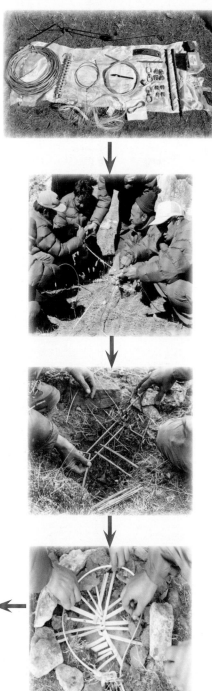

How do scientists know when a snow leopard, or any animal, has stepped into a trap? Each trap is connected to a small hidden radio transmitter which sends a special signal to satellites and radio receivers. A slow, steady radio signal indicates the transmitter is working well. When a trap is sprung, our receivers beep urgently. We also receive text messages and email on our mobile phones and computers telling us exactly which trap has sprung. This is very important so that we can get to the trap as quickly as possible and begin work. The most important part of trapping any animal is safety. We must make sure the snow leopard is freed from the trap as soon as possible to minimize any danger to it.

Over the next two weeks, we set thirty traps in different locations, all within one hour's easy jog from our camp. Then the waiting begins. Each day our team visits diffrent traps to make sure everything is working well. The days turn into weeks. We wait, always ready to leap into action when a trap is triggered.

19

The Himalaya are full of all sorts of wonderful animals. Sometimes we accidentally trap the wrong ones. Sometimes we catch domesticated yaks, sometimes, like here, a wild blue sheep. It is always dangerous work freeing these thrashing, frightened animals, but we succeed each time.

After nearly three weeks of false alarms, something triggers a trap high on a mountain pass. Thankfully it is daylight, and our team responds immediately. As we approach the trap site, we expect to see horns of a blue sheep or a yak—our usual catch. But this time we find something very different. The icy green eyes of a huge Tibetan grey wolf stare back at us. This species of wolf has never been seen in this part of the Himalayas. A big achievement for science in Nepal to have discovered it here!

20

There is no way we can approach this magnificent but angry wolf without tranquilizing it. Once we dart it with our dart gun, the wolf falls asleep within twenty minutes. We free it from the trap and make sure it is uninjured. We lay the wolf on level ground and back away to wait for it to wake and return to the wild. Wolves are an important part of any ecosystem. Skillful hunters, they keep populations of other animals healthy by preying on sick and old blue sheep, deer, marmots and pikas.

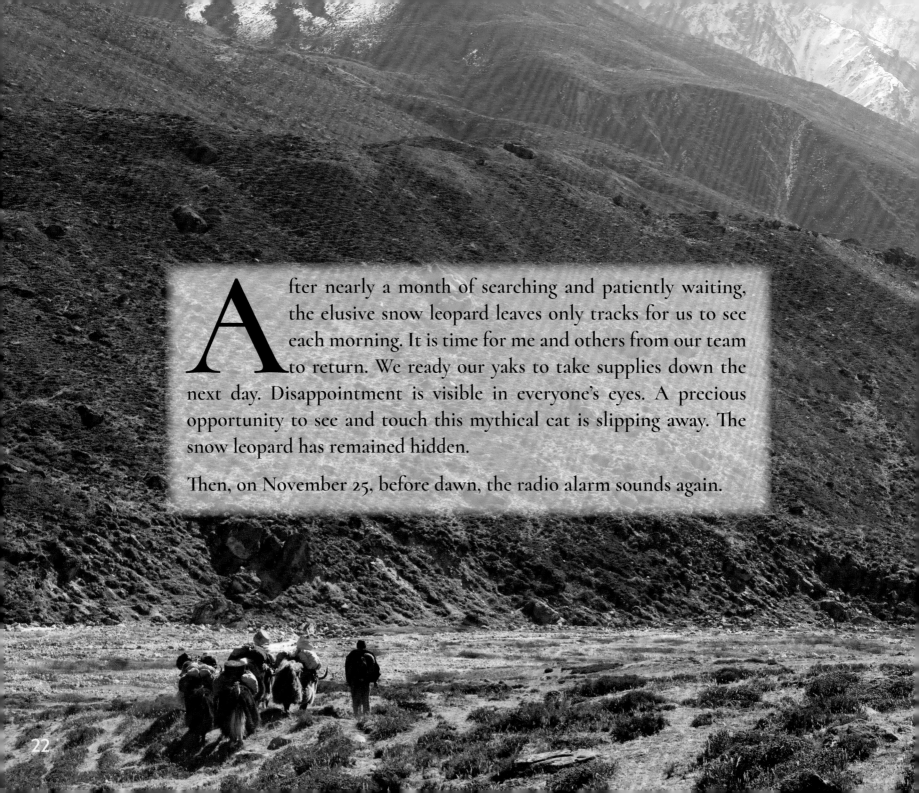

After nearly a month of searching and patiently waiting, the elusive snow leopard leaves only tracks for us to see each morning. It is time for me and others from our team to return. We ready our yaks to take supplies down the next day. Disappointment is visible in everyone's eyes. A precious opportunity to see and touch this mythical cat is slipping away. The snow leopard has remained hidden.

Then, on November 25, before dawn, the radio alarm sounds again.

November 25. Our radio transmitter alarm has triggered!

Each breath of icy Himalayan air scrapes our lungs as we push higher. Most of us know this is our last chance to encounter the snow leopard. My heart beats wildly from the climbing and the excitement of not knowing... We round a crag, and...

Morning sunlight reveals the face of a snow leopard. We stand and stare. Huge, yellow eyes aflame with fear and anger stare back at us. A silent snarl reveals sharp, white fangs.

We shake off our awe; there is work to do. Anil, the veterinarian, loads his tranquilizer gun with a dart that will put the snow leopard to sleep, just like the wolf, so we can work on it without danger to the cat or ourselves.

Furious, the snow leopard leaps about, pulling hard on its trapped paw. We worry it will hurt itself.
We cannot take a shot without the cat sitting still, so we wait for it to calm down.

Slowly it tires, until finally it exhausts itself and stares at us with a look of angry resignation.

Anil takes a shot! It hits home perfectly in the lower thigh of the snow leopard's back leg.

After fifteen minutes the snow leopard is still, lying on a steep slope. We use a ski pole to gently tap it to make sure it is really asleep.

L ed by our lead biologist Rinjan, our team springs into action. We see immediately that it is a large, young male. The first step is to remove the cable from his leg and check to insure the limb is undamaged. It is!

Rinjan places a stint in the mouth of the snow leopard to protect its tongue from unintentional movement of the sharp teeth. Then we fit the collar gently around its neck—neither too loose nor too tight.

The sun has come up and we cover the eyes to protect them while we finish attaching the collar.

W e check the teeth and claws to make sure no injuries have occurred.

All in perfect shape!

The chance to study a snow leopard in the wild is rare. We collect a sample of its fur and its blood for later study. We then measure the length of the snow leopard and weigh him. He is roughly 41 kilograms, or 90 pounds.

Once we have finished our measurements, we load the snow leopard onto a stretcher and carry him to a safe location for waking up.

ll our work has taken only twenty-five minutes. We give an injection of medicine that will slowly wake the snow leopard from his sleep.

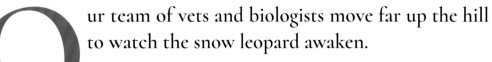
Our team of vets and biologists move far up the hill
to watch the snow leopard awaken.

Slowly he regains consciousness. He begins to stand up, unsure of himself as the drug begins to wear off. His muscled body amazes us. The snow leopard takes his first steps back into the wild.

Though it will take some time for him to get used to this new collar, it is worth it. The temporary discomfort he may feel is a small price to pay for the long-term conservation benefits wearing such a collar will bring to all snow leopards.

By tracking our leopard's movements, scientists will gain a rare glimpse into his secret life. This will help us better understand how to protect all snow leopards from hunters and a changing climate.

• • • • • • • • • • •

The snow leopard collared on November 25, 2013 was named Kangchenjunga after the great mountain that towers above all forms of life in this part of the Himalaya. He wore his collar successfully until Sept 2015. During that time, this strong, young snow leopard made four trips back and forth from Nepal to India. In both countries he hunted blue sheep, looked for mates, played with his friends, drank from mountain streams and slept in caves. Several times he came very close to crossing into China. On one of his long walks he climbed to nearly 20,000 feet on a glaciated mountain. This was the highest recorded climb of a snow leopard.

All of Kangchenjunga's movements appear as black dots on our maps. They are GPS waypoints, which are transmitted from his collar to a satellite orbiting earth and back to our computers.

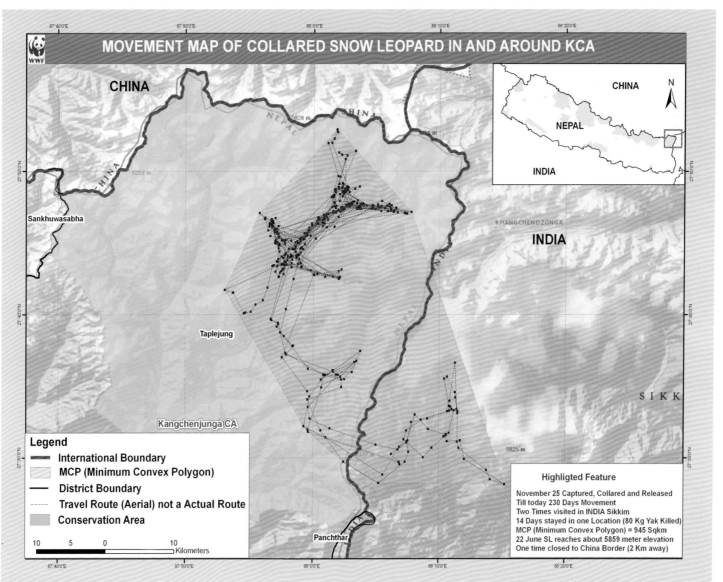

MOVEMENT MAP OF COLLARED SNOW LEOPARD IN AND AROUND KCA

CHINA

NEPAL

INDIA

CHINA

NEPAL

INDIA

Sankhuwasabha

KHANGCHENDZONGA

INDIA

Taplejung

SIKK

Kangchenjunga CA

5825 m

Legend
━━━ International Boundary
▨ MCP (Minimum Convex Polygon)
── District Boundary
----- Travel Route (Aerial) not a Actual Route
▨ Conservation Area

10   5   0   10
                  Kilometers

Panchthar

Highligted Feature
November 25 Captured, Collared and Released
Till today 230 Days Movement
Two Times visited in INDIA Sikkim
14 Days stayed in one Location (80 Kg Yak Killed)
MCP (Minimum Convex Polygon) = 945 Sqkm
22 June SL reaches about 5859 meter elevation
One time closed to China Border (2 Km away)

Nearly 22 months after we collared Kangchenjunga, the automatic release activated and the collar dropped off in the neighboring state of Sikkim in India. We have since caught photos of Kangchenjunga in camera traps roaming collarless in his mountains. We have shown that Kangchenjunga, and likely others in the area, consider their home to be parts of Nepal, India and probably China as well. We plan to collar more snow leopards in the Kangchenjunga area to gain deeper understanding of their habits so we can perfect our ability to protect them.

Our commitment to protecting snow leopards and other animals of the Himalaya will never end. But that's okay. We love our work. As for our Kangchenjunga, he's out there somewhere living out his life proud and free among the greatest mountains in the world.

WWF Nepal began in 1967 and works in close partnership with the Government of Nepal and local communities to protect wildlife including elephant, tiger, rhino, red panda and of course the snow leopard. WWF Nepal seeks to protect complete ecosystems which often span international boundaries. This approach ensures important ecological processes are able to continue.

The events in this book took place in the Kangchenjunga region of Nepal, which straddles the Himalayan border between Nepal, India and China. For over twenty years WWF Nepal has worked for the protection of the entire Kangchenjunga mountain ecosystem including its glaciers,

grasslands, rivers, human communities and the animals and forest that thrive there today.

The snow leopard sits at the top of the wildlife food chain in the high Himalaya. The continued survival of snow leopards in the Kangchenjunga area is due to the hard work of the governments of all three countries that share this sacred mountain. Yet, it is the people who call the forests and alpine meadows of Kangchenjunga region home, that we need to thank for the snow leopard's survival. Its fate is in their hands.

For more information on WWF Nepal, please go to *www.wwfnepal.org*.